The World
of
Soft Edges

by
Barbara Boncek

Crazy Ladies Press
229 Main Street
Kingston, NY   12401

Acknowledgments

Acknowledgment is gratefully given to the following publications in which some of
these poems originally appeared:

Oxalis, The Alchemist, Trust, The Poetry Peddler, Bitterroot, and Crazy Ladies/ Wise Women.

"River Fear" won first place in the Walter H. Memorial Award of the Florida State Poetry Association.

"Mama" won Honorable Mention in the *Times Herald Record* contest

"Butter Words" first appeared in the Stone Ridge Poetry Society's Poetry Calendar.

"A King" won first prize in The Hudson Valley Writers contest

I wish to acknowledge the care and support of my husband, Louis, and the technical support of my daughter, Marianna Boncek, and son, John Boncek.

Much Madness is Divinest Sense
Emily Dickinson

Crazy Ladies Press
Shirley Powell, Editor

ISBN # 0-9710021-1-1

This book is dedicated to

Inez Gridley

my teacher and mentor for over forty years

and to

Shirley Powell

who brought my dream to fruition.

CONTENTS

The Cloak 1

Women Weave and Men Fish 2

The Wail of Fate 3

Rain Walk 4

River Fear 5

Smack 6

Lollipops 8

White Poverty Blues 9

Lies 10

Prospective Buyer 11

The Evolution of Islands 12

The Retreat of the Blue Bloods 13

Desert Storm 15

After the Stroke 16

Paint the Damn House 17

These Magical Lenses 18

Mama 20

Brown Soldiers 21

Vintage Caruso 22

Simple Fare 23

Corn Rows 24

Miracles 25

A King 26

Lineage 27

Butter Words 29

Razor Strop 30

Pungent Reminder 31

Civilities 32

Looking Sideways at God 33

The Crooked Cross 34

The Encounter 35

The Dancer 36

43 37

The Wind is Old 38

West Wind 39

Chant Before Sunset 40

THE CLOAK

Come,
wrap yourself
in the light
cloak of night.
Feel its satin lining
slide over your fears.
Leave the frustrations
of dying days
and come with me
into the world of soft edges
and moon silence
of dew baths
and fireflies.
Come,
wrap yourself
in the light cloak of night
and enter the realm
of reflection.

WOMEN WEAVE AND MEN FISH

"Women weave and men fish,"
my father said leading me
for the first time
to "our" boat.

In spite of the gray day
I was alive with excitement.
"Ah, Seamus, today you become a fisherman,"
my brothers said
slapping my back in camaraderie.

We rowed only a short distance
when my stomach began to roll
my mouth filled with spit
and my knuckles became white lumps.

"Hold on, Seamus, hold on!"
my brothers shouted
but with each rise and fall of the waves
my stomach turned inside out
and I fell to the bottom of the boat
sick, sea sick.

That night
my father carried me home
and threw me on the bed.

"Is he dead?" my mother cried
"Is he dead?"

"He might as well be!"
my father said
turning his back on me.

And so I became
a maker of looms
the finest looms in all Mayo
looms on which
women weave.

THE WAIL OF FATE

Ah, shame on you
Seamus O'Moran
dying before the fight
had begun.
I counted on you
to carry the banner of Mayo
like your ancestors
before you
but you had to impress
the lassies
by drinking the bottle dry
so that when you stood up
in the wagon to wave goodbye
you pitched forward
and broke your bloody neck.

Your poor mother, Bridget,
cried her eyes blind
but no amount of tears
or prayers
could bring you back.
And your crippled father, Thomas,
sat by your casket
for three days and three nights
like a cold stone.

Listen to the keening, Seamus,
Can you hear them
wailing over your dead body?
'tis a comfort to the mourners
and the likes of me
who can not
will not weep
    not now
    not yet.

3

RAIN WALK

They tell me
    I was born in a haystack
    just as the storm broke
    and my first comfort was not
    the arms of my mother
    but a bath of warm rain
    that washed me clean of birth.

They tell me
    my father wrapped me
    in his sweat-wet bandana
    and brought me to the house
    leaving me on the cool parlor floor
    while he returned
    to the hayfield for my rain soaked mother
    whose moans forced him to leave us
    in search of a doctor.

They tell me
    as sick as my mother was
    she tried to comfort me
    by stripping away the bandana
    and wrapping me in a rag rug
    and between her sobs
    she hummed lullabies
    until I fell asleep.

I do not tell them
    that my night dreams
    are full of sobs
    and when a summer storm breaks
    I walk in its warm rain
    humming lullabies.

RIVER FEAR

When I was two
I fell from the bridge
and the river caught me
cradled me in a bed of silt
where my father found me.

Racing time and death
he carried my limp
blue-faced body home
to my grandmother
who breathed sweet breath
and prayers into my cold lungs
again and again
until the blue faded
and a pink tinge appeared.

"A miracle!" pronounced the doctors.
"She has recovered unscathed."

But that's not true.
Though I swim and dive
in man-made pools
I never swim in the river
never go near it.
I am afraid it will catch me
cradle me in its bed of silt
and never let me go.

SMACK

When I closed my eyes
I saw myself
as an eight year old
sitting in the front pew
of Mt. Carmel Church
with the rest of the Confirmation Class.

On a signal
from Sister Margaret Mary
we rose and approached the Bishop.
"Remember your Confirmation name,"
the nun whispered.
"And don't be surprised
when the Bishop taps
you on the cheek."

Though intimidated
by the pomp and heavy incense
I stepped forward smiling.
When the Bishop asked for
my Confirmation name
I proudly answered, "Catherine."

The color drained from his face
and his eyes narrowed.
"Catherine it shall be,"
he said as he smacked me
across the face.
Yes, smacked
not slapped
not tapped
smacked!

Sister Margaret Mary
froze momentarily as did
the altar boys, the deacons,
and sub deacons.
Recovering more quickly
than the rest of us,
she led me from the altar
back to the front pew
where I sat suffering
more from the sting
of embarrassment
than the actual smack itself.
I would not and did not cry.

The smack was the talk of the town,
the clergy, and the nunnery.
Gossip, rumor, and innuendo flourished.
Who was Catherine?

Only the Bishop knows.

LOLLIPOPS

They are too busy
to come to the Christmas Play
or the Easter Pageant
but when I come home
there is always
a package of lollipops
on the kitchen table.

They never ask about
the play or the pageant
only
"Did you find the lollipops, dear?"
"Yes, thank you."

Alone in the empty house
I sucked them all
into sweet slivers
that cut my tongue.

WHITE POVERTY BLUES

I'm suffering the blues
white poverty blues
pick at my bones.
No jobs
no money
no food
no respect
and what is a man
or a woman
without respect?

They're nothing!
'Cause poor
is their fault
their sin.
They're nothing!
'Cause poor
has no respectability.

LIES

I remember the lies:
Santa Claus and the Tooth Fairy
and of course, Prince Charming.
I held on to that one for years.
And Happily Ever After
What a laugh!

But I understand
their perpetuation.
They're shards
of hope
we keep
like amulets
crystals or
scapulars
to protect ourselves
when lives
leech
despair and
desolation.

PROSPECTIVE BUYER

A stranger
I walk through
your house
opening closet doors
see
a white
satin
negligee
hanging
between
the suits
and jackets
smile
and you
do too
as we
move on
to other closets.

THE EVOLUTION OF ISLANDS

You and I
were a continent
solid, indestructible
so secure were we
that we paid no attention
to the small fissures
appearing here and there.
Normal we thought,
nothing to worry about
but after a particularly hard winter
a crack appeared.
We were concerned
but not really alarmed.
Then a cataclysmic rupture
ripped us apart
leaving a strait
of uncharted waters
between us.

Poor swimmers and boaters
we never dared
to cross the strait.
So we drifted apart
became two separate entities
islands
beacons.

THE RETREAT OF THE BLUE BLOODS

When the day
grew heavy with humidity
and the kids crankier by the minute,
I drove them to the top
of Denman Mountain
where the blueberry bushes
were ripe and ready for picking.

The shade of the maple and oak
cooled and calmed us
and we began to laugh
and clown around
filling our pails and our mouths
full with juicy berries.

"We're blue bloods,"
cried my oldest
as he stuck out
his blue tongue.
"Blue bloods,"
mimicked the youngest
whose face and shirt
were smeared with berries

Our laughter was interrupted
by a loud crash.
Coming toward us
was a big brown bear.
The kids turned to stone
their faces as gray as granite.
"Don't run," I whispered.
Oh God, don't let them run!
"Walk. Walk slowly backward"

For a moment
neither the bear nor the kids moved.
"Walk backward," I hissed.

Like little wind-up robots
they began to move backward
step by step
single file.
To our left we saw two cubs
merrily munching berries
totally oblivious of our presence.
"Keep walking," I encouraged.
"Keep walking."

When we reached the car,
I yelled," In, everybody in!"
The robots turned into circus clowns
tumbling over each other as they
scrambled into the back seat.
As I slid into the front seat
I let out a sigh of relief

From behind me
my oldest whispered in my ear.
"Mama, were you scared?"
"Scared? Honey, I was
absolutely terrified!"
"Absolutely terrified!"
mimicked my youngest blue blood.

DESERT STORM

Oh, desert wind
I need you
to blow the sand
from his bones.
Let a foot protrude
    a hand
    an arm.

I need some part of him
to put in a casket
and bury in solid ground.
I don't want a foreign desert
to be his grave.

I want him here
in this rural cemetery
between his father and grandfather.
I want his son to come
and lay flowers on his grave.
I want a place to kneel and grieve.

Oh, desert wind
blow the sand from his bones.
Let a foot protrude
    a hand
    an arm.

AFTER THE STROKE

Often, I tried to write this poem
but the words would not come.
They were trapped behind a blood clot wall.
I could not coax them out.

When blood thinners were prescribed
they ate away at the foundation.
The wall crumbled
words tumbled out
a river of words: juxtaposition
exacerbate, solidus, and its twin, virgule.
Even hubris, arrogant as ever,
joined in the words rush.

Not all the word came back.
Some died.
But, with the aid of a dictionary,
I have resurrected enough of them
to write this poem.

PAINT THE DAMN HOUSE

Paint the damn house!
Hide the scars and sores.
Suffocate the yesterdays
one brush lap at a time.

Paint the damn house!
Paint it white with black trim
a second time bride
with nailed down shutters
behind which bats sleep.

Paint the damn house!
Hide the aging secrets.
Layer on a new life
one brush lap at a time.

THESE MAGICAL LENSES

I'm afraid of them
but when I put them on
I can see.

Trees are no longer
blurs of green
they have leaves
delicately veined
and perfectly formed.

The clock in the tower
has slender hands
that give out time   free
to those who can see.

When I look at people
I can see the lines
in their faces
and if I look
directly into their eyes
I can see the color
yours are green
flecked with brown.

With these magical lenses
I can see
subtle changes in expression
frowns beginning to form
even yawns stifled.

At times I see too much
twinges of pain
flashes of anger
jealously even distrust.

That is why I'm afraid
of these magical lenses
afraid that someday
when our faces
are leathered and lined

and our hair is gray
I might see you flirting
then openly courting death.

I will try desperately
to hide my jealously
my anger   my fear
but I will not
discourage the affair.
I will not leave you.
I will be at your side
helping you to accept
and embrace her.

But if some day
I look directly
into your green eyes
flecked with brown
and see your love for me
dying   slowly dying
then I will take off
these magical lenses
and become blind.

MAMA

Mama,
Mama rise up
out of that casket
and wrap your arms
around me
like you used to do
when all we ate
was love
ladled over stale bread

wrap your arms
around me
like you used to do
and feed me
the only dessert
we ever had
hope
mounded high
on white plates
trimmed in yellow.

Mama,
Mama rise up
and teach me again
that poor
is not a sin
and death
is not the end.

BROWN SOLDIERS

No one
but Papa
ever picks
the brown dahlias
standing like soldiers
around the edge of the garden.

Only Papa
walks among them
lifting heads
and bracing crooked spines.

When he comes upon
a tall straight one
with its head up
he cuts it down
and places it
in a bucket of water.

Inspection completed
he gathers the cut ones
into magnificent bouquets
and takes them to church
where flickering candles
highlight the stalwart beauty
of Papa's brown soldiers
sent to guard the sanctuary
as they did the garden.

VINTAGE CARUSO

Papa seldom sings
except in church
or when he drinks
too much wine.

Then his deep baritone
can be heard
beyond the house.

Mama tries
to shush him
which only makes him
sing louder
not in English
but his native Slavic.

In the morning
he tries to avoid the neighbors
who thank him
for the unexpected concert.
"A real Caruso," they say.
Embarrassed, he mumbles,
"too much wine,"
and leaves quickly for work.

Mama smiles
as she watches him go.
then turns to begin
her daily chores
softly humming
Slavic ballads.

SIMPLE FARE

Grandma raised them out back
as a hedge against hunger
and when times got really hard
we had them twice a week
over homemade noodles.
But we never called them squab.

They were pigeons, fried pigeons
and we didn't dine on them either
we ate them with our fingers
sucking the butter from the small bones
and lapping up what was left
with hunks of homemade bread.

I can still taste them
smell them
feel the brown butter
greasing my chin.

CORN ROWS

Casket planted in corn rows
across the Plains
    Little Phoebe in Kansas
    John in Nebraska
    and Sarah
    beloved wife
    lies beside
    The Santa Fe Trail.

Drained of desire
he fled to California
where he harvested
a bumper crop of golden kernels.
"Rich! You're rich!"
the Forty-niners shouted
watching him put golden nuggets
in corn rows
    one for Phoebe
    one for John
    and one for Sarah
along the Santa Fe Trail.

MIRACLES

I want you to rise
like Lazarus
but you never believed
in miracles
often saying
"There's no such thing!"
You live.
You die."

And then you began to die.

I held your hand
read to you
and when you cried
I wanted to die
with you
but death was yours
alone.

I stand over you now
wishing I were a Jesus
but you never believed
in miracles.

A KING

Though no royal blood
runs through his veins
he knows he is a king
and his sons know

how he tamed
the tangle rooted prairie
and turned it into
a sea of wheat
that burned black
in one lightning afternoon
and his sons know
in the black stubble
he found courage uncharred.
In the spring he planted
its seed with the wheat
and when the leaves shouted
the season, he gathered wheat
but his sons harvested courage.

And though no royal blood
runs through his veins
he knows he is a king
and his sons know.

LINEAGE

Ignoring the squalor
surrounding her
she sits propped up
against an overflowing
garbage can
smoking a cigarette.

"Pardon me, señora,
may I take your picture?"
Her earth brown eyes
survey every inch of me
before she answers, "Sí."

Carefully snuffing out
the unfinished cigarette
she struggles painfully to her feet
rearranging the tattered shawl.
Slowly she folds the red blanket
she was sitting on
and places it rakishly
on top of her head
during all this activity
her face is devoid of emotion.

But when I say, "Ready?"
she straightens her shoulders
turns sideways
lifts her chin ever so slightly
and stares into the camera.
The late afternoon sun
casts a glow
over her face
revealing the aristocratic
high cheek bones
and the long straight nose
of an Aztec matriarch.

I snap several Polaroid
and give her one.
She holds it at arm's length

then draws it close
studying every detail.
"That me?"
"Yes, that's you."
"No, not me."
She makes the Sign of the Cross
and kisses the picture.
"That my mother
and she is with
God."

BUTTER WORDS

I bask
in the
golden glow
of your butter words
melting over me
until they reach
my scrapes and scratches

then I remember your butter
is lightly salted.

THE RAZOR STROP

He is hanging from life
    an old razor strop
    an ornament
    an antique.

No one ever touches him
or sharpens ideas
on his leathered wisdom.
He hangs alone
on the hook of age.

THE PUNGENT REMINDER

I buried him
but when I got home
the smell of him
permeated the house
his clothes
his pillow.

So I buried him again
in the clean smell
of bleach and pine
but on the first damp day
the smell of him rose
from the cracks in the floor
a pungent reminder
death can not be buried.

CIVILITIES

Like a basketball
small civilities
are bounced back and forth.

"Hello!"
"How are you?"
"Fine thanks and you?"

Then the slammer
catching me off balance.
"He died last week."

I try to recover
but the ball slips through my fingers
and rolls into the street

where I watch it
come slowly
to a dead stop.

LOOKING SIDEWAYS AT GOD

Sundays we look sideways at God
If we look straight ahead,
we'll miss Carrie Alston
wearing the latest mod dress
up to her knees
and down to her navel.

Old Mr. Young can tell you
just how far up and how far down
Carrie's dress goes
though he says he has no idea
who she is.

Aunt Henrietta and her cronies
are convinced
Carrie's going to walk
naked into Hell
greeted by half this congregation.

Of course no one admits
looking sideways.
Only God can see
their righteous eye balls
rolling from side to side.

THE CROOKED CROSS

I hang from him
like an odd earring
a miniature cross
swinging from his long lobe
I suppose I should be happy
swinging free like that
instead of strung out
on his necklace along
with all the other
freaky symbols
but I just know
that one of these days
I'm going to catch
on his coat collar
and rip off his lobe
he'll be so damn mad
he'll crush me under his boot heel
I'll lie there
and wait for someone
to pick me up
someone who needs
a silver cross
even if it is
a little crooked
and dripping blood.

THE ENCOUNTER

The blue heron rises from its rookery
as a king rises from his throne
and with the same elegant grace
soars upward to survey the marsh
then slowly descends
and when its long thin legs
touch down in a small stream
the bird collapses its umbrella wings
to stand knee deep
in fish-filled water.

I dare not breathe
as I watch this majestic bird
dine on the delicacies of the stream.
Satiated, the heron
steps forward on hinged legs.
It is then that the bird sees me
and instantly becomes a blue stone.

Afraid it will fly away
I, too, remain motionless
barely breathing
until the shriek of a vulture
startles us both.
Stretching its elongated neck
the heron searches for the intruder
then rises spreading its wings wide
and soars across the marsh
to the safety of its rookery.

THE DANCER

For a long time
I lie awake
listening to your
rhythmic breathing
    inhale-one-two-three
    exhale-one-two three.

I slip out of bed
and begin to waltz
    round and round
bare feet noiseless
on the carpeted floor.

I swirl into a time
of innocence and hope
when your arms were muscle-filled
and I was a slender sapling
bending to your pressure.

Spinning past the mirror
I see an image I do not recognize.
I twirl back for a second look.
In the moonlight mirror
is a wrinkled reality dancing
to the rhythm of time

    inhale-one-two-three
    exhale one-two-three.

43

I was 43
once
and
remember
none
of it
not even
the birthday
itself.

But then
I don't remember
33 or 27
even 55 is lost.

It's hard
to believe
I forgot
living through
all those years

But I'm told
it's not uncommon

that as I grow older
I will forget the todays
and remember the yesterdays.

I wonder
will I
remember 43?

THE WIND IS OLD

The wind is old
    a contemporary
    of time
    and creation.

It blew hot
across forming continents
rose over new oceans
and circled the poles.

The wind is old
Before Adam
it wandered through Paradise
kissed the apple
cooled the snake

and when Adam appeared
comforted him
long before Lilith
and Eve.

The wind is old.
It hovered over
horrific battlefields
mingled with mushroom clouds
seeped into the hovels
and hide-a-ways of the world.

The wind that today appears
young and fresh
is an old wind
old as time
old as creation..

WEST WIND

I call to the West Wind
and it comes
leaping like a leopard
circles
and then
by a command not mine
lies down at my feet.

CHANT BEFORE SUNSET

I come early
before the sun sets.

It is here
on the highest spot

that I will marry
with the moon.

Its fullness
will envelop me

and I will follow it
across the sky

unafraid.

ABOUT THE AUTHOR

Barbara Boncek lives with her husband, Louis, in Grahamsville, New York where she taught social studies for seventeen years. Her poetry has appeared in many small literary magazines and journals. She is presently writing chapbook reviews for the on-line magazine *Frigate: The Transverse Review of Books.*